BOOK INFORMATION

Copyright 2014 by A. Herbert Jordan.

ISBN Number: 978-1500685942
Library of Congress Control Number:
2014913711
First Edition
Printing 10 9 8 7 6 5 4 3 2 1
January, 2015

Cover design by Hicham Aziz

All rights reserved. No part of this publication may be reproduced, distributed, or transmitted in any form or by any means, including photocopying, recording, or other electronic or mechanical methods, without the prior written permission of the publisher, except in the case of brief quotations embodied in critical reviews and certain other non-commercial uses permitted by copyright law.

Persuasion Magic is available in print and electronic editions.

1

Special discounts are available on quantity purchases by corporations, associations, and others.

For details:
http://bigbusinessbenefits.com/contact-us/
Or e-mail ahjordan@bigbusinessbenefits.com.

Note: The bold halftone print indicates a hyperlink in the electronic version of this book.

DEDICATION

I dedicate this book to David Bianchi CLU, and Jim Annis.

Both of these men are superb salespeople and organization builders who consistently place, "Service Above Self," and use their talents to make the world a better place.

I also dedicate this book to long time friends Ron and Joy Kern.

Ron and Joy, I appreciate your positive attitudes and everything that you have done for me, and my family.

TABLE OF CONTENTS

ACKNOWLEDGMENTS

About two years, my daughter gave me a copy of *To Sell is Human,* and it fit so well with my own philosophy that I decided to write my own—totally different—book. My first acknowledgment, therefore, is to:

Daniel H. Pink: author of several New York Times bestsellers, including *Drive: The Surprising Truth About What Motivates Us* and *To Sell is Human: The Surprising Truth About* Moving Others. (http://danpink.com)

A special thank you to Elizabeth Sheppard and Stephen Hughes.Thank you for taking the time to review many drafts of my work and provide honest, constructive critiques.

Also, I owe a debt of gratitude to all of the ethical salespeople and non-salespeople in the world, and to the researchers, authors, and reporters who have helped to explain what makes people tick.

INTRODUCTION

One person's idea literally lit up the world.

On July 29, 1878, Thomas Edison was fishing on the shores of Battle Lake, in what is now known as Wyoming. While he was waiting to observe a total eclipse of the sun, he examined his bamboo fishing pole, pulled a few threads from it, and had a "Eureka!" moment that involved using bamboo as a filament for a light bulb.

His insight came as the result of many unsuccessful previous attempts to produce a commercially viable lightbulb. One that would generate a pleasing light, have an acceptable life span and be affordable.

Edison's realization enabled him to create the first practical light bulb, where many others had failed. Luck combined with years of experience. In fact, Edison said, "I have not failed. I've just found 10,000 ways that won't work."

Also, Edison was able to capitalize on his realization because he solicited backing for his company, the Edison Electric Light Company, to produce economical electricity to power the lightbulb. His backers included J. P. Morgan and the members of the Vanderbilt family.

What's the lesson here? Edison moved people to become involved in his success. He proposed his ideas for adoption, and they did get adopted. Edison knew how to create the team synergy that was needed to bring a major innovative product to market in less than two years.

Persuasion Magic is a tool that you can use to enlist the aid of others so you can catapult your ideas to adoption. You already know the answers. This book will help you to realize them.

WHY THIS BOOK ENGENDERS SUCCESS

> *The value of an idea lies in the using of it.*
>
> -Thomas Edison

A boy and a girl are walking along the beach in, let's say, Atlantic City, NJ. The girl goes over and picks up a starfish. She hurls it into the ocean. The boy just looks at her. The girl picks up another starfish and throws it in, then a third, fourth, and eventually a hundred starfish. All the while the boy watches her, but says nothing. Then he asks, "Why are you doing this?"

"I'm saving their lives," says the girl.

"But there are so many of them stranded on the beach; I can't see how it can make any difference."

The girl hurled one more starfish into the ocean. She watched it ride on a wave and then disappear under the surface of the water. "Made a difference to that one," she said.[1]

You may have an idea that makes a worldwide difference like Thomas Edison, or you may have an idea that makes a difference in the lives of a few, like the girl with the starfish. It doesn't matter. Your idea deserves to be considered, and this book will help it become so.

---

[1] This is a motivational story that many orators have used in speaking engagements and as a part of a sermon.

> *"Pretend that every single person you meet has a sign around his or her neck that says, 'Make me feel important.' Not only will you succeed in sales, you will succeed in life."*
>
> — *Mary Kay Ash*

Persuasion Magic empowers non-sales people to discover how to pinpoint and convey the benefits of ideas that they would like to see come to fruition.

It also makes it easier for salespeople to convey the benefits of products or services.

If you're concerned about making certain that your ideas get adopted, or if you need to close more sales to beat quota, don't worry. This book will help you to formulate the insights and answers that you need.

In fact, *Persuasion Magic* is likely to be the one book that you highlight the most in your entire library (except for some of your college textbooks). As you read it, you'll see many things that make you say, "ah-ha," to yourself. Solutions that have been never obvious will be become evident, like pieces of a puzzle snapping together. You will realize that you know how to move others to want to support your ideas.

I have a request. When you're considering the meaning of this book, please think of the informal definition of "magic"—wonderful and exciting, as in "a magic moment." Also, I'm making an assumption. I'm betting that you genuinely feel that the person (or group of people) you want to persuade will benefit because good things will happen. This book is about moving people, not manipulating them. To borrow a term from software developers, this book is about "white-hat" techniques—the things that the good guys use.

I'll bet you're a bit like me; there's hardly a week that goes by where I'm not trying to influence or persuade someone (a co-worker, boss, child, zoning board member, etc.) to adopt one of my ideas. At this point in my life, I'm not involved with selling on a day-to-day basis, but I'm constantly involved in marketing and non-sales efforts.

To see just how common non-sales presentations are, let's explore a finding by Daniel Pink, author of The New York Times #1 Bestseller, *To Sell is Human: The Surprising Truth About Moving Others.*

Mr. Pink conducted a valid statistical analysis of more than seven thousand full-time adult workers in the United States and discovered these two main points:

1. *People are now spending 40 percent of their time at work engaged in non-sales selling— persuading, influencing, and convincing others in ways that don't involve anyone making a purchase. Across a range of professions, we are roughly devoting twenty-four minutes of every hour to moving others.*

2. *People consider this aspect of their work crucial to their professional success—even in excess of*

the considerable amount of time they devote to it.[2]

Since there are times in our lives when we are all dedicating our energy to either selling a product or service or promoting our ideas, concepts, and conclusions, it makes sense to make that aspect of our job as easy and enjoyable as possible.

Persuasion Magic empowers you to look within yourself and find your little light (the passion) so that your efforts in sales and non-sales situations move people.

On any given day, you're likely to find that only two or three of the gems in this book will motivate you. As the situations in your life

---

[2] Daniel H. Pink, *To Sell is Human: The Surprising Truth About Moving Others*, New York: Riverhead Books, 2012, 21.

change, your reactions will evolve. Review[3] this book again in two or three weeks and you'll have a different experience than you have today.

Part One, "My Golden Words," helps you to put yourself in the place of the person whom you're trying to persuade. There are six questions or short exercises. When you finish answering them you will have a much better understanding of how to garner support.

Part Two, "Almost Magic Phrases," consists of a series of questions and phrases that I use to understand the needs of others. I invite you to use them too. Once you have the answers to even one or two of these questions, you'll be more effective when you attempt to convince someone to support your efforts.

Part Three uses affirmations to build self-

---

[3] I said "review this book" instead of "read this book," because reviewing it implies that you think about its content. You know yourself better than anyone. Each time you consider this book's content, you'll come up with different, often better, solutions.

esteem and fuel enthusiasm.

Part Four features constructive questions specifically designed to help you view the world from a different perspective.

Parts Five, Six fSeven use short poetry to help you examine how you want to promote your ideas, and banish negativity.

Finally, there are **four appendices** that are specifically written for salespeople.

What would your reaction be if I claimed that we are all salespeople? I know that if someone told me that, my reaction would be something like, well that's a bunch of BS. But Daniel Pink changed my attitude. In *To Sell is Human* he states:

> The *What You Do at Work?* Survey begins to provide a richer portrait of the twenty-first-century workforce, as exemplified by the world's largest economy. The existing data show that 1 in 9 Americans work in sales. But the new data reveal something more startling: So do the other 8 in 9. They too

are spending their days moving others
and depending on their livelihoods on
the ability to do it well.[4]

This observation brings us to a discussion of one the biggest obstacles for sales and non-sales people alike, "call reluctance."

The material in *Persuasion Magic* instills pride and perspective to salespeople who are experiencing call reluctance.[5]

Although I have only anecdotal evidence, I have found that many salespeople can ruin their productivity for an entire day, or longer, if someone (a customer, prospect, sales manager,

---

[4] Daniel H. Pink, *To Sell is Human: The Surprising Truth About Moving Others*, New York: Riverhead Books, 2012, 24.

[5] It's easy to find evidence of sales call reluctance in large sales bullpens—typically two or three salespeople will be killing time, employing creative strategies to avoid making cold calls. (Click here to view a list of many books on the subject of sales call reluctance.)

fellow salesperson, etc.) makes them feel that they are being sleazy or inconsiderate.

People with jobs as diverse as an accountant, artist, computer programmer, prison guard, writer, actor, statistician, or truck driver have ideas that they want to see implemented, but are reluctant to take action. Often, the ideas that they are reluctant to promote wilt away because there is insufficient follow up. Sadly, many non-sales people may have been just one sentence away from seeing their ideas adopted, just as numerous salespeople are often one step away from closing a sale.

> *Consult not your fears but your hopes and your dreams. Think not about your frustrations, but about your unfulfilled potential. Concern yourself not with what you have tried and failed in, but with what is still possible for you to do.*
>
> *- Pope John XXIII*

Creativity is allowing people to come up with new solutions. *Persuasion Magic* is, in essence a prism that makes it easier to view the world from different perspectives.

> *Creativity is just connecting things. When you ask creative people how they did something, they feel a little guilty because they didn't really do it, they just saw something. It seemed obvious to them after a while. That's because they were able to connect experiences they've had and synthesize new things.*
>
> *- Steve Jobs*

Use your creativity to focus on moving people so that your ideas and goals are realized.

A. Herbert Jordan
January, 2015

P.S. If you're viewing this book on an electronic device, (phone, computer, tablet PC, iPad, etc.)

it is easy to search for a word or phrase such as, "Ironic," and focus on the bit of humor or inspiration in a creative way. (For an example, try searching for the poem, "Ironic." If you're reading a printed version, turn to page 180.) Take a look now. After you read the poem, you'll probably smile.

Printed versions provide enough space to record insights, draw, or paste in a photo or a picture that you may have clipped out of a newspaper or magazine.

Having a place to record my thoughts makes it easy to go back and review the personal inspirations that made the day feel better. Sometimes, just glancing at a meaningful personal insight can improve my mood for an entire day, or even a week. Perhaps it will work for you too.

This page is for your thoughts, drawings, poems, etc.

This page is for your thoughts, drawings, poems, etc.

PART 1: THE "MY GOLDEN WORDS" SELF INTERVIEW

> *"The art and science of asking questions is the source of all knowledge."*
>
> *- Thomas Berger*

"You live under my bed?" Suzy asked, amazed. She peeked under the bed to see what might be under it, but saw nothing unusual.

"Yes," said Karrit. Are you going to eat me?"

"Why would I want to eat you?" asked Suzy.

"Everyone knows that the monsters that live on top of beds eat all sorts of strange things," said Karrit.

- *The Monster on Top of the Bed*

In this children's picture book that I wrote, two children who consider each other potential "monsters" strive to get to know each other. Eventually, by employing the principles of The Golden Rule, they become best friends.

Although they don't know it, they are engaging in non-sales selling—they are selling the fact that they have the potential to be the other child's best friend. They are building a relationship.

In a way, building a relationship is selling your potential to be a friend. The first step in building a business friendship is to develop a clear understanding of the other person's needs and desires. The second step is to understand how you can help them to achieve their goals.

I use questions and short exercises to help me build an expanded understanding of that person's needs and desires. Six of them are in this book.

I am then able to warmly interact. It's easy for me converse in a friendly, positive manner. Perhaps you will also find my questions and exercises useful.

1. DESCRIBE IN EIGHT (8) WORDS OR LESS THE IDEA YOU WANT TO HAVE ADOPTED, OR THE PRODUCT OR SERVICE YOU WANT TO SELL.

2. *USE EIGHT (8) WORDS OR LESS TO FINISH THIS STATEMENT: MY IDEA (PRODUCT, OR SERVICE) WILL HELP TO INCREASE PRODUCTIVITY BECAUSE* _____

3. PLEASE FINISH THE FOLLOWING STATEMENT IN SIX (6) WORDS OR LESS: MY IDEA (PRODUCT, SERVICE) WILL REDUCE HASSLES BECAUSE _____

4. *LIST THE JOB TITLES OF EACH CATEGORY OF PERSON WHO WILL BENEFIT WHEN YOUR IDEAS ARE IMPLEMENTED, OR YOUR PRODUCT OR SERVICE IS PURCHASED.*

5. DESCRIBE, IN TWELVE WORDS OR LESS, SOMETHING THAT THE PERSON ADOPTING YOUR IDEAS OR PURCHASING YOUR SERVICES OR PRODUCT HAS TO GAIN.

6. *EXPLAIN HOW YOUR IDEAS (PRODUCT OR SERVICE) WILL PROVIDE A SOLUTION FOR THREE CHALLENGES — TECHNOLOGICAL, FINANCIAL, EMOTIONAL.*

This page is for your thoughts, drawings, poems, etc

.

This page is for your thoughts, drawings, poems, etc.

PART 2: ALMOST MAGIC PHRASES

> *"I've learned that people will forget what you said, people will forget what you did, but people will never forget how you made them feel."*
>
> *- Maya Angelou Honored poet, civil rights leader and essayist in a 2012 interview for Beautifully Said Magazine*

It's been my experience that before I can persuade someone to adopt my ideas or to buy a product or service from me, I need to understand their needs and their feelings.

The following phrases are based on integrity. The answers to these questions help me to relate to people. They also help me to pinpoint out the advantages of my concepts, products, and services.

In some cases, I've written a brief explanation about why I use the phrase, or how I use it.

In some cases I'll propose two phrasings: one for non-sales situations, and one for sales situations. I'll enclose the alternate delivery in (a set of parenthesis). [Square brackets] indicate an alternative scenario, such as "stopping by" instead of "calling."

Initial Qualification

- Would implementing (buying) _____ fall into your area of responsibility?

  If the answer to this question is, "no," then I'm speaking with the wrong person, and I need to find the right person.

- Could you tell me . . .? This is a non-threatening phrase.

  If the answer is, "no," then I need to find out why they can't tell me. The answer could be that they don't have the correct knowledge base, or it could be because of security concerns.

- The reason I'm calling [stopping by] is to acquaint you with my idea (myself and my company) and, possibly, to get some direction. When I meet with people, I find that they often want to know why I'm there.

  This short phrase tells them why I stopped by or called, and it conveys the fact that I'm interested in knowing their thoughts, and following their advice.

- I'm looking for ___<Contact Name>___.

  Use this simple phrase when you're speaking with an Operator/Attendant and want to reach an important person quickly. It's the type of phrasing that the C-Level officer of a company uses when they place a phone call to a subordinate.

PROBING

- Is there anything I can do to expedite things?

   If the answer is, "yes," then follow the advice you're given. If the answer to this question is, "no," accept the fact that you may have to wait unless you have another contact who has the ability to instruct, or influence, others.

- Is it/that possible?

   This is a simple question. Listen carefully to the answer. You may find yourself being educated.

- If we had received the green light last week, what would I be doing today?

This phrase is a good way to help the person (or panel of people) you are speaking with visualize your suggestions as being implemented.

- I'm really excited about the possibilities. Is there anyone else who I should contact?

This statement/question pair conveys enthusiasm on your part and then explores how you can expedite the adoption of your ideas or purchase of your services or product. It's also useful when you are concluding a job interview.

- Who else do you know that might benefit from _____ ?

- Would it be appropriate to get together soon?

- What obstacles do I need to overcome to implement this idea (get this order)?

- What else can I do that will help you (your company) say, "Okay, let's do it?" or "We'll give your company a try?"

- Would it be appropriate to touch base   with
  _____?

- Can you give me an idea as to when you'll be making the decision?

- Would it be possible to make a three-way call? It would save you the trouble of calling back. Also, if others have questions, I can answer them directly. You won't be put in the middle.

- Could you give me a little insight into _____?

- What else can I do to earn your business?

- Could you suggest someone else who might be interested?

- I can be as relevant as possible. Can you give me an idea if ___ <a question that you'd like answered>?

ARRANGING AN APPOINTMENT

- We've gone over a lot of information. I'd like to get my thoughts together, then go over them with you. Do you want to set up a time to get together?

- What do I need to do to convince you to give me the go ahead (a trial order)?

- I'll fit everything into a one or two-page letter. Would it be better to e-mail, snail mail, fax, or drop it off?

- If you'd like, I'd be pleased to get you some written information. Would that be appropriate?

43

(Pause) Would you like me to drop it off? I can be there around ___<time>_____ on ___<day>_____.

- *(Say, "Respectfully," only if it feels right.)* Respectfully, we should get together. We can do the job for you.

- Can you share your insights with me? What would motivate you to say, "Okay, let's give it a try?"

- Frankly, I make a better impression in person than on the phone.

- I'd like your business. What do I need to do to earn it?

- Can we set up a time to get together?

Or

- When's the best time to get together?

- Could we set up a meeting, or *(with a humorous tone)* would it be appropriate to ask for the order now?

- From the information that we've shared, I feel our _____ will benefit you. Could we get together?

- I'm sure we can do a great job for you. Can we get together ___<day>_____?

- Can we get together __<day or time> _____?

TRANSITION

- I've sent a brochure (letter of explanation), but it will be much more meaningful when someone goes over it with you.

- You're really going to be delighted that we decided to get together.

- I understand.

- From what you've told me, you'd benefit from _____. Here's   why:

- Some people find it easier to understand the literature when someone goes over it with them.

- Sometime over the next six months I'd like to see this implemented (earn your company's business).

Six months is generally a long enough period to allow someone to feel that no pressure is being exerted. However, sometimes it's best to change "six months" to "a year," or some other time frame.

UNCLASSIFIED

- Would it be okay if I mention your name when I call ___<name of person>_____?

- Thank you. You've been very helpful. *(Slight pause, and reflectively)* I'll let you know what happens.

- We've gone over a lot of information. Would you mind if I ___<ask for what you want> _____?

- Will you be there?

- Will that be appropriate?

- Would you prefer information that is . . . as relevant as possible? *(Follow up by saying you want to send relevant information, and ask qualifying questions.)*

- We've gone over a lot of information. I'd like to put my thoughts together and then get back to you.

- From what you've told me . . .

- If it's not being too forward, ___ <make a request>_____.

- *(To recap)* I say all this to ___<summarize what you want>_____.

- I'll touch base with _____ later. Thanks.

PART 3: AFFIRMATIONS FOR SELLING, LIVING AND PERSONAL ENERGY PRODUCTION

"I think I can. I think I can. I think I can. I know I can."

-The Little Engine That Could

When I was a child, I used to love to hear my mother read *The Little Engine That Could*, a book by Watty Piper that teaches the value of optimism and hard work. In the story, a small train climbs a mountain and succeeds because it kept telling itself "I think I can, I think I can. I think I can. I know I can."

As I grew older the story never left me. Eventually, I started to write my own affirmations—affirmations that were meaningful to me. I have at least 367 affirmations that I value.

I use these affirmations in conjunction with my constructive questions. The affirmations act as an inoculation against negative thinking. They are very specific, and I trust that you will find them helpful.

To comment on an affirmation, or submit one of your own for possible publication, please visit http://bbb.max-opp.com/contact-us/feedback-on-stimulating-sales-success-affirmations-for-selling-living-and-personal-energy-production/.

This page is for your thoughts, drawings, poems, etc

This page is for your thoughts, drawings, poems, etc.

1. *I AM SELF-RELIANT.*

2. I REACT WHEN IT IS APPROPRIATE.

3. *I ANTICIPATE THE EFFECT OF INEVITABLE CHANGE.*

4. *I LIMIT THE SCOPE OF MY CONCERNS.*

5. *I PROOF MY WORK BEFORE PRESSING <SEND>.*

6. *I TRUST IN THE CAPABILITIES OF OTHERS.*

7. I LEVERAGE MYSELF WITH TECHNOLOGY AND PEOPLE.

8. *I TAKE TIME TO ENJOY MOMENTS OF INSPIRATION.*

9. *I ALLOW MYSELF TO RELAX.*

10. I FULFILL DESIRES — MY OWN AND OTHERS'.

11. *I KEEP MY MIND OPEN AND RECEPTIVE TO NEW OR ALTERNATIVE IDEAS.*

12. *I ACTIVELY SEEK SYNERGISTIC SOLUTIONS.*

13. *I VISUALIZE OUTCOMES AND WORK TOWARD THOSE I WANT TO REALIZE.*

14. I RECOGNIZE THE VALUE OF OTHER PEOPLE'S PRIORITIES.

15. *I USE IDEAS AS A SPRINGBOARD FOR DISCUSSION.*

16. My LIFE IS FILLED WITH CELEBRATION.

17. *I HAVE SUBSTANTIAL SPIRITUAL, FINANCIAL, SOCIAL, AND EMOTIONAL RESOURCES.*

18. I STAY CONNECTED TO BUSINESS AND SOCIAL CONTACTS.

19. *I RECOGNIZE WHEN IT IS EASIER TO DO SOMETHING THE "HARD" WAY.*

20. *I TAKE ADVANTAGE OF NEGATIVE FEEDBACK.*

21. *I BELIEVE IN MYSELF!*

22. *I RECOGNIZE VIABLE SOLUTIONS.*

23. *I USE MY TIME WISELY AND EFFECTIVELY.*

24. *I RECOGNIZE THE VALUE OF DOING SOME THINGS SLOWLY.*

25. *I UNDERSTAND THE VALUE OF TRANSITION.*

26. *I AM INTELLIGENT AND INTUITIVE, AND I USE THESE TRAITS TO MY ADVANTAGE.*

27. I UNDERSTAND AND APPRECIATE THE MESSAGES MY BODY SENDS ME.

28. I HELP OTHERS TO RECOGNIZE THEIR FULL POTENTIAL.

29. *I AM SERENE BECAUSE I FLOW WITH THE UNIVERSE.*

30. I PRIORITIZE WELL AND TAKE APPROPRIATE ACTION.

31. *I RECOGNIZE THE VALUE OF INTERIM GOALS.*

This page is for your thoughts, drawings, poems, etc.

This page is for your thoughts, drawings, poems, etc.

PART 4: CONSTRUCTIVE QUESTIONS

Ask and you shall receive.

- Various places in The Bible

These constructive questions are part of a larger collection of constructive questions.

The answers to these constructive questions help me to find solutions that I can implement. Finding an acceptable solution makes me feel better about myself.

I consider a destructive question something like, "Why can't I make friends?" From my perspective, the answer to a destructive question makes me feel worse about myself.

The combination of constructive questions and affirmations is a powerful, valuable way to counteract negative self-talk.

I invite you to jot down your answers to these questions, draw a picture, or paste in a photograph that's meaningful to you.

To comment on a constructive question, or submit one for possible publication or provide feedback on the affirmations, please visit feedback on the constructive questions please visit: http://bbb.max-opp.com/contact-us/feedback-on-stimulating-sales-success-constructive-questions/.

1. WHEN I GET TO WHERE I'M GOING, IS THAT WHERE I WILL WANT TO BE?

2. *IF I WEREN'T WORRIED, WHAT WOULD I DO?*

3. WHAT ENVIRONMENTAL FACTORS HAVE CHANGED?

4. IF I LOOKED AT THIS PROBLEM FROM A 30,000 FOOT VIEW, WOULD IT MAKE A DIFFERENCE?

5. WHAT ARE THE ADVANTAGES OF OTHER POINTS OF VIEW, AND HOW CAN I INCORPORATE THEM INTO MY SOLUTION?

6. AM I LOOKING FOR A SYNERGISTIC SOLUTION?

7. HOW DO I CREATE OPTIONS IN THIS SITUATION?

8. IF I WERE TO LOOK BACK ON THIS SITUATION IN FIVE YEARS, WHAT WOULD I FIND HUMOROUS ABOUT IT?

9. DO I NEED TO DEVELOP PERSPECTIVE?

10. *WHAT IS THE BEST WAY TO GO ABOUT SOLVING THIS PROBLEM, WHILE STILL ENJOYING MYSELF IN THE PROCESS?*

11. HOW CAN I CONVERT THIS FEELING OF UNCERTAINTY INTO A FEELING OF CHALLENGE?

12. WHERE IS THE SMILE IN THIS SITUATION?

13. WHAT DO I NEED TO FEEL RENEWED?

14. WHAT OTHER OPTIONS ARE AVAILABLE?

15. IF I WERE TO LOOK AT THIS SITUATION FIVE YEARS FROM NOW HOW IMPORTANT WOULD IT SEEM?

16. WHAT AM I OVERLOOKING?

17. ARE THE GOALS THAT I SET BEFORE STILL RELEVANT?

18. MIGHT I FEEL DIFFERENTLY ABOUT THIS DECISION TOMORROW?

19. WOULD A DISINTERESTED THIRD PERSON DRAW THE SAME CONCLUSION?

20. WHO DO I KNOW WHO CAN HELP ME WITH THIS?

21. AM I BEING TOO DEMANDING (INCONSIDERATE) OF MYSELF?

22. IF I WEREN'T AFRAID (CONCERNED, RESTRAINED BY CIRCUMSTANCES) WHAT WOULD I DO?

23. WHAT ENVIRONMENTAL FACTORS HAVE CHANGED?

24. AM I REPEATING MISTAKES THAT I HAVE MADE IN THE PAST? (IF SO, WHAT STEPS CAN I TAKE TO CHANGE THE SITUATION?)

25. HAVE I CONVEYED THE THINGS THAT I'VE DONE RIGHT LATELY TO MYSELF (MY SPOUSE, MY EMPLOYER)?

26. AM I LOOKING FOR A CREATIVE (INNOVATIVE, UNIQUE) SOLUTION?

27. DO I FEEL THIS WAY BECAUSE MY EXPECTATIONS HAVE BEEN VIOLATED?

28. MIGHT I BE JUMPING TO AN INAPPROPRIATE CONCLUSION?

29. WHAT WOULD I NEED TO FEEL CERTAIN (MORE CAPABLE, HAPPY, CONFIDENT)?

30. AM I REACTING OUT OF FRUSTRATION (FEAR, ANGER, HABIT, OLD PATTERNS)?

31. WHAT WOULD I NEED TO FEEL UNDERSTOOD?

32. *IF I WERE MORE FLEXIBLE, HOW WOULD I FEEL ABOUT THE SITUATION?*

33. DO I ASK FOR WHAT I WANT?

34. AM I FOCUSING ON NEGATIVES OR POSITIVES?

35. WHAT WOULD HAPPEN IF I TRIED TO NURTURE, INSTEAD OF CHANGE, THIS PERSON?

This page is for your thoughts, drawings, poems, etc.

This page is for your thoughts, drawings, poems, etc.

PART 5: MOTIVATIONAL SALES POETRY

> *Poetry is when an emotion has found its thought and the thought has found words.*
>
> - *Robert Frost*

I invite you to read these poems silently, or read them aloud; examine them in sales meetings, and discuss them with your prospects and clients.

Before you read the poems in this section, let's discuss the word, "Motivational."

Not every poem in this section is designed to make readers feel good; they are written to encourage one to look within themselves, and uncover reasons to:

- Realize the value of timing;

- Communicate more effectively;

- Put more prospects in the sales pipeline;

- Take some time to have fun;

- Get off your tush and make phone calls;

- Etc.

I'd appreciate receiving your comments, and any poems that you wrote to motivate yourself. If you're reading a printed book, the best email address   is aherbertjordan@bigbusinessbenefits.com. Please include the name of the poem in the subject line. Or, if you're submitting a poem that you written, the word, "Poem", followed by a colon, the title of the poem, and your name. For example:

Poem: "Lighthouse Soul" by Joan Davies

1. A SUPERB SALESPERSON

A superb salesperson is:

A prism
breaking the light from each prospect, each
customer
into beauty
for all to see.

Each color
a want or need.

An artist
complementing those colors
adding form and substance
to complete the sale.

2. CELEBRATE AND INOCULATE

Use my poems to:

entertain

empower

motivate

yourself

your staff

wherever

whenever

They:

elicit smiles

banish fears

break down barriers

Enjoy them as you would:

A hot shower in the morning
A cool breeze in the afternoon
A twinkle in the eyes of a loved one.

3. LISTENING MEANS

Being willing to
hear someone

Their meaning, not their words.

When I change my agenda
from what I want to hear
everyone has something interesting to say.

When I listen *and respond*
selling is:

easier
enjoyable
exciting!

4. SLUMPS

It's a kick, making a sale
a natural high
almost narcotic

Slumps steal that high
sap my energy
make me wonder, doubt

Activity
doing something
anything
pays off.

5. A SALESPERSON'S PRAYER

God, please grant me:

The skill to help
The challenge to grow
The autonomy to act and
The wisdom to know when I should.

6. Disturb and Resolve

Help someone move forward
that's what selling is all about

Nevertheless,

When I place each prospect's
needs and desires
above my own,
I am a professional.

7. WAITING FOR A BIG DEAL TO CLOSE

I reach for the phone
but know better

pushing won't help
I've done all I can

the best thing to do
is to find
new prospects.

Who knows?

One might make
my "Big Deal"
look small.

8. THE PIPELINE

I approach many prospects

When I've only got one
he *has* to be good.

With many,
some can be good
some not so.

9. LABELS

Labels can mislead
especially
when misinterpreted.

Names are labels

Until I know about the person
or the firm
I try not to assume.

10. GOING TOO FAR

"Today is the first day of the rest of your life."

Wonderful Native American saying.

When I'm out to beat quota
I sometimes adapt it:

This hour is the first hour of the rest of my life

This minute is the first minute of the rest of my life.

However

"This second is the first *second* of the rest of my life."

That's breaking things down too far.

11. BREATHE DEEPLY

Ten times a day
from your lower lungs

That's an Rx
for more energy.

Not that you need it.
Just in case.

12. SALES IS MENTAL WORK

So what?

So when nothing seems to go right

do something physical

Let your mind take a vacation.

13. OPPOSITIONAL

Not me.
Can't be.

I'm so flexible
I require starch to stand up.

Not me.
Can't be.

What's right is right.
I can prove it!

Not me.
Can't be.

Uh-oh
I just listened to myself.

14. HIGH HOPES

Sinatra
Rams and dams
Ants and rubber tree plants.

Songs
Fantasy -- Reality
Failure -- Success

Sales
Dreams -- Plans
Omission -- Commission

Solve for
the line between
Positive Mental Attitude and
wishful thinking.

144

15. VOICEMAIL

Can be:

frustration or expedition

anger or delight

yes or death

Depending upon
attitude and technique.

But I'd still like to shoot
all of those automated attendants.

16. TIMING CAN BE EVERYTHING

When an idea does not work
reschedule it.

17. FOR BEST RESULTS

Ask simple questions

Listen to each answer

Blend

Set aside

Reply.

18. TO ACHIEVE A BREAKTHROUGH

Communicate!

19. THE DIFFERENCE BETWEEN

Suspects and prospects is:

Desire
Immediate need
Money

Given time
Everyone is a prospect

But

Who has eternity to
close a sale?

20. SELLING IS A PROCESS

Selling
is a process

that needs to be done
one step at a time
in a timely manner

Unless

my prospect tells me
to go right to the bottom line.

21. OUTDATED?

I understand what you want
but you're going to buy what I want to sell
you...

Just doesn't cut it anymore.

(Not that it ever did.)

22. ENTHUSIASM

Doesn't always sell, but

When's the last time you wanted to
buy something from
some guy or gal
who was bored with their job?

23. *I'm Making a List*

Of the things I need to say and do

To make people happy

For me and for you

It occurs to me that this list

Should not need to exist.

Should and should not

Need not be done

Perhaps better guidelines

Are happiness and fun.

24. SOMETIMES

The difference is

>One word
>One thought

Contrast:

>I will make it work

>I need it to work

>I want it to work.

25. *SHOULD YOU GO FOR IT?*

Imagine yourself a unicorn
your head held high
music streaming from your horn.

You're flying across the sky
through two rainbows.

Imagine you've drawn this
picture on the canvas of your soul
with the caption
Believe in the magic of your dreams.

Now, decide.

26. A PROSPECT'S THOUGHT BUBBLE

Please, just tell me

What do you want?
How can I help you help me buy?

Then I'll decide

Do I want to help you?
Do you want to help yourself?

27. RELATIONSHIPS

Relationships are
made from Gossamer threads

that can have more strength than steel or
be as fragile as
a spider's web.

I strive for the former.
My clients appreciate that.

28. CLOSING

Is often as simple as

asking someone for the order

Then keeping my mouth shut

for the sixteen years
until my prospect responds.

29. FUN PROSPECTING

Some days calling on prospects

makes me feel like a kid.

Crunch, crunch, crunch

crunch, crunch, crunch

through the snow

Crunch, crunch, crunch

crunch, crunch, crunch

I do go.

30. OPTIMISTIC PERSPECTIVE

An optimistic sales person

does not see the glass of life

as being half full instead of half empty.

The optimist knows

the glass will always be refilled.

31. THE WAVY LINE THEORY

When I can't draw a

perfectly straight line.

I don't try.

I draw a wavy one instead.

Everyone thinks it is supposed to be that way.

32. COLD CALLING

Cold calling can feel so frigid
especially over the phone
until someone says, "yes."

Suddenly the world is warm again
I'm proud, glad that I dialed those
numbers.

I close my eyes
breathe deeply
savor the warmth of the moment
for the next time that
my fingers pause over the buttons.

33. THE TROUBLE WITH PHONE CALLS

Is that I don't have any clues
except what I hear
and that's not always a lot.

I think I'll go to the mall.
Walk around the parking lot.
Look in the cars.

What's that I see in the
three-year old Ford Taurus?
A baseball glove
Two pink baby seats.

Sounds like a prospect for

term life insurance.

I reach into my portfolio
Write on a reprinted ad for
$250,000 of term insurance
I show the math

Two-hundred-fifty-thousand dollars
times two percent
equals five thousand dollars

About one hundred dollars a week,
forever
if you die.

The two babies and the ball player
will appreciate that.
KL5-3252 – Call me. I'm Joe.

With my phone

I take a picture

of the annotated ad

Capture an image of the car

Walking away, I drop the ad in
through the Ford's slightly cracked
window.

I move on to the pink Cadillac

See two briefcases with tags — Linda
and Lois.

I pull out an ad for partnership
insurance.

Write:

$500,000 to

buy out the business

if one of you dies

With my money, not yours.

KL5-3252 – Call me. I'm Joe.

I put the ad on the Caddy's window

move on to a four year old Buick.

I'm Joe!

34. SOMETIMES I OBSCURE

Sometimes I obscure proposals
hide behind the details

Best I can figure out is
I'm afraid someone will say, "yes."

Maybe, I don't feel it's 100% right
for my client.
Or,
Maybe, it's not right for me.

Sure glad it doesn't happen often.

35. OUT OF DATE

"Always be closing"

Worked back when

Salespeople held all the cards.

Now, when prospects have

instant access to information

it's more like

"Always be inviting."

I invite prospects to discover

the advantages of buying.

It's not like the old days.

I facilitate their journey.

36. SPREAD WARMTH

A smile

coupled with a
sincere inquiry and
listen, listen, listen

actively.

Nothing makes a prospect feel warm and
fuzzy like listening to them.

37. I THINK OF MYSELF AS A FILTER

I think of myself as a filter

that allows suspects and prospects to pass through, but

slows the flow of prospects.

Then

Prospecting is a matter of

observing who is

Traveling without hurrying.

38. POUND IT OUT

When I'm in between sales

I pound clay

Get rid of all my aggressions.

Convert my creativity into shapes.

I mold myself while I mold the clay.

Literally and figuratively.

It's wonderful

to step back

as an artist (a salesperson) and

admire the things that I've achieved.

39. *IT'S TRUE, LEONARD COHEN*

God is alive, magic is afoot

Alive is afoot, magic never died.

How could it?

Magic surfaces

every single time

a salesperson

makes a sale.

This page is for your thoughts, drawings, poems, etc.

This page is for your thoughts, drawings, poems, etc.

PART 6: SHORT STUFF FOR THE SPIRIT

> *Breathe-in experience, breathe-out poetry.*
>
> *- Muriel Rukeyser*

The short poems in this section always put a smile on my face, and I'm delighted to share them with you. I like all of them, but I must admit that my favorite poem is "Ironic." It brings back fond memories of my dog, Twigs.

To comment on any poems, or submit a short poem for Short Stuff for the Spirit, please visit: http://bbb.max-opp.com/contact-us/feedback-on-stimulating-sales-success-short-stuff-for-the-spirit/.

1. TODAY IS THE FIRST DAY OF THE REST OF YOUR LIFE

Today is the first day of the rest of your life.

The REST of your life.

The rest of your LIFE.

The rest of YOUR life.

2. AN RX FOR OVERLOAD

Shift your focus.

Do something fun.

Let the back of your mind find the solution.

It doesn't mind working overtime.

3. *IF YOU TOOK*

If you took all of the people in the world
and lined them up one-after-the-other

You'd find bureaucrat's heaven.

4. IRONIC

I want to get in,

while the dog wants to get out.

For exactly the same reason!

5. WHEN IT ABSOLUTELY

When it absolutely, positively will not
work,
look at it from a different perspective.

6. WHAT'S ON THE GROUND

What's on the ground

can't fall down.

7. MILK AND COOKIES

Milk and cookies

peanut butter too.

These are things

I eat at the zoo.

8. FINISHING UP

Finishing up makes room

Emotionally.

Financially.

Spiritually.

Besides, we all know,

Nature abhors a vacuum.

This page is for your thoughts, drawings, poems, etc.

This page is for your thoughts, drawings, poems, etc.

PART 7: POETRY IN THE KEY OF LIFE

The only journey is the one within.

- Rainer Maria Rilke

"I was watching the news and a man was killed by an airplane. It crashed on him as he was shoveling snow. I learned my lesson the easy way. I don't shovel snow." This brief story was told to me by Ronald Kern, over thirty years ago. (Ron and Joy Kern are two of the people to whom I've dedicated this book.)

The story puts a smile on my face every time I shovel snow, but the reason I'm including it here is because it shows a little bit of the strange things that happen in life, and the ways that they can inspire humor.

These poems provide a deep peek into my soul.

My first inclination was to exclude them, but I

187

decided that motivation is inspired in many different ways.

For example, the first poem, "Moment by Moment," explores the way that I sometimes feel when I don't think I'm making progress in a sale, or in life. I've decided to share it because I've discovered that a number of people who are selling a product, or trying to convince someone to implement one of their ideas, identify with my feelings. When they find that I have felt this way, they don't feel as isolated and alone. The same is true for my poem about procrastination, "Help It's S-p-r-e-a-d-i-n-g."

"Season Shift" is a beautiful Haiku poem. It makes me happy, and I want to share it.

The poems about my father and mother are included to pay homage to them. Also, I used to sell life insurance. It would be a special pleasure if life insurance salespeople find that these two poems open up avenues of conversation that are conducive to helping their clients realize the value of estate planning and life insurance.

To comment on, provide feedback, or submit a poem for potential publication, please visit http://bbb.max-opp.com/contact-us/feedback-on-stimulating-sales-success-poetry-in-the-key-of-life/

1. MOMENT BY MOMENT

i.

I feel . . .

Supreme, as I create

from the depths of my soul

Everything I'm doing is right

Flowing

Dictated by experience

Facilitated by God

"How could anyone not like this?"

It's good

Great

Superb

Fantastic...

... a small voice proclaims, "It's a first draft."

ii.

I explain –

My soul pouring out

It's not what he wants

    Shock

    Dismay

    Anger

    Disbelief

    Denial

    Denial

    Denial . . .

. . . a timid voice calls out "Next time, listen." iii.

I feel . . .

Worthless. Utterly worthless.

A waste of space.

A loser,

with no talent.

Investing time into projects that

- have no value
- rehash failures

If I died now –

- no one would miss me
- the world would . . .

. . . I hear myself proclaim, "Wait out the

moment."

iv.

I am grateful for

Snow covered mountains that glisten their

beauty

A rainbow in a single drop of rain

The sweetness of silence.

v.

I deserve more!

If I don't stand up for myself . . .

vi.

Dumb.

I am so dumb.

Won't I ever learn?

. . . If anyone but myself talked to me this way, I'd walk out the door.

2. *THERE'S NO WAY I CAN PROVE*

That a positive attitude makes life better, but

I sure know that

Looking at the down side of things

Makes me feel a whole lot worse.

3. A PRAYER

Spirit of thanks

empower me.

Lift up my heart

let me feel all the gladness

Fly with the wind

rise with the sea

spin with the world

move within me.

Spirit of thanks

make yourself known

lift up my heart

help me to be.

Spirit of thanks

empower all

empower me

I'll give to thee.

4. *HELP IT'S S-P-R-E-A-D-I-N-G*

The clutter.

It's gone beyond the office

Into the family.

Clothes on the sofa.

Papers on it too.

Piles on the entertainment center.

The bedroom is starting to feel stale.

Dishes are in the sink. Not many. But some.

Soon, they'll be more

Unless I take action.

I've been on overload.

Put off things.

Said, "I'll get to it."

Now, I'm paying the price.

Nothing feels good.

I enjoy a clean house.

Don't necessarily like to do it.

Guess it's time

to straighten things up.

Get that fresh smell back

199

into the house and

into my life.

5. HONESTY

It's hard,

To lay my soul on the line

An escalator for others to step on

Interestingly,

When I do it

People usually use the stairs.

6. A SQUIRREL'S FREEDOM

When I was a kid

I trapped a squirrel

In our shed.

Induced it in

Fed it nuts everyday

Built up trust until

One day it entered the shed.

Slam went the door.

It ripped the shed to pieces.

When you take away freedom

Life gets ripped to pieces.

7. LIZ PUTS PEANUTS OUT FOR THE SQUIRRELS

The shells are better for the lawn

Better than the sunflower seeds I would throw.

Some people give from their hearts.

Others from their souls.

8. SEASON SHIFT

Crisp air makes breath show.

Bear begins to hibernate.

Fall into winter.

9. IT WOULD BE

My father's birthday in two days.

I don't have to buy a card.

Kind of silly, sending a card to a dead person.

I mean, how can they possibly open it.

I believe you can read this, even as I'm typing.

I feel the stream of love that is coming out my heart

Can reach up to Heaven and give you a little nudge.

If you can read this, Dad, you know I love you.

You can sense the tears in my eyes and you can see me typing

H-A-P-P-Y B-I-R-T-H-D-A-Y!

P.S. Give my love to Mom too.

10. MARION

Meeting someone with my mother's name

is special.

Never failing to bring back memories of

    Auburn hair

    A love of life

    Rides

    in the country

      down the shore

      up the Poconos

around the block.

    And so much more.

She passed away in '69.

Memories that once drew tears

Now bring

Smiles,

Silent prayers and

Self confidence.

APPENDICES FOR SALESPEOPLE

You don't close a sale; you open a relationship if you want to build a long-term, successful enterprise.

– Patricia Fripp

The information in this section is addressed toward the needs of salespeople, but if you are in non-sales, simply adapt it to your needs.

APPENDIX 1- A RELAXED WAY TO APPROACH THE PEOPLE IN PURCHASING

"They're all morons," said Wallace Trask to Tricia Goldman, a fellow salesperson.

"I haven't found that to be the case."

"Really, they are. Always concerned with rules—not with the needs of the company's employees."

To Tricia's dismay, Wallace continued to vent, and the conversation went on for another four minutes while Wallace described all of the ridiculous rules that Purchasing had imposed on him.

When Wallace left, Tricia picked up the phone and called the Purchasing Manager at a Fortune 500 company.

She touched base with Martin Heldwig, and said, "Martin. Tricia Goldman, over at Trisafe. Have you had an opportunity to review the paperwork I dropped off last week?"

"I've looked it over, but I haven't given it a thorough review," replied Martin, a smile in his voice.

"Could you give me an idea on the next step that I need to take to qualify as an approved vendor?"

"I think the next step would be for you to speak with Geraldine Brookline; she's one of our attorneys. She had a couple of legal questions that need to be addressed. Once you get her approval, I'll be able to finish the certification process."

"I'd be happy to do that. What's the best way to contact her—email, phone?"

"Her direct number is (617) 555-8323. Tell her I said to call, and ask her to reference vendor application number X232F17."

"Great. I'll let you know what happens."

"That's fine, but there's no need. When she approves the paperwork, I'll be notified, and then I'll be in touch with you."

"Super. Thanks so much."

"My pleasure."

As the above dialogues imply, it is often necessary, or advantageous, to approach the professionals in a company's Purchasing Department. Most of the phrases in this book are generic. They work as well as when you speak with a purchasing agent or purchasing director as they do when you conversing with a sales manager. There are also some phrases that should be used only when you are speaking with a purchasing professional.

Here are a few phrases that you might use:

1. **"Which users (managers) do you feel I should speak with?"**

When you ask this question, most purchasing professionals will either provide you with a list of names or explain why they feel it is not in your best interest to call end users directly.[6]

---

[6]I suggest that whenever a Purchasing Agent refers you to an end user or manager, you use the recommendation to your best advantage by saying something like, "Hi, my name is Cliff Mavers. We've never spoken before, but Harry Snellenberg suggested we touch base."

2.   **What's the best procedure to be included on your approved (preferred) vendors list?"**

Asking this question helps you to be placed on the bid list and receive a Request for Proposals.

3.   **Can you give me a feeling how I (we) compare with other vendors who...**

Use this phrase to gain information to be used in your proposal.

4.   **What do I (we) need to do to get our first P.O.?**

Don't be shy about asking this question. Many sales are made because a salesperson showed ardent interest in the sale.

5.   **What's the best time to reach
     __<contact's   name>___?**

*Trying to reach a busy person who
does not you can be a time-
consuming process. Asking this
question can give you the
information that you need to get
through more quickly.*

6. **Somewhere over the next three-to-six months, I'd like to earn your company's business.**

Contrast this statement to "I'd like to pick up an order and check next week, if possible." Is one week to make a purchase decision reasonable if you have never even met the person? It might be, depending upon the circumstances and your prospect's level of urgency, but the request may seem threatening if it is used prematurely. On the other hand, the phrase "three-to-six months" does not pressure your prospect. You really can do things to earn a prospect's business over that period. Do not be concerned about losing business if your prospect needs to act sooner. When prospects have an urgent need, they explain them. Unfortunately, with most prospects, you will need to develop urgency.

APPENDIX 2 - ENLISTING THE ACTIVE SUPPORT OF ADMINISTRATIVE ASSISTANTS AND SECRETARIES

Many successful salespeople say that getting the sponsorship of administrative assistants, secretaries and other support personnel, helps to get appointments. Conversely, novice salespeople often describe obstacles that stopped them from "getting past" a secretary or other gatekeeper.[7] Do you agree with these statements? Please consider this: If either of these assertions is true, it makes sense to do everything you can to impress administrative assistants and support personnel favorably.

I submit that you are most likely to gain a support person's full cooperation when

---

[7] The term "gatekeeper" is used to describe someone whose job is to prevent you from getting in to see someone, unless your presence is deemed beneficial.

you show respect for their responsibilities, duties and position. Instead of trying to get past your initial contact, point out the reasons why complying with your request make sense. Explain how speaking with you will provide a benefit.

Please take a moment to reflect upon the best approach when you speak with an executive secretary whose job description includes restricting access to well-known associates and elite people who have a good reason to speak with him or her. (That is a good reason, from the administrative assistant's supervisor's point of view.)

I suggest that you tell the truth, phrased in the most positive way. Do not try to intimidate the contact, or falsely imply that you are a close friend. Let's look at a typical cold canvassing situation. Please assume that you:

1.   Do not know anyone else within the organization.

2.   Are selling a product that has much competition

3.   Were referred to this decision maker by the Operator after using an introductory statement suggested in this book.

Assume that the decision maker's administrative assistant asks your name and company name. She also probes to uncover the reason that you are calling. Assume that she has been instructed to (very politely) tell anyone that her boss will call them back, if he is interested. What can you possibly say to get her boss to speak with you?

You might be surprised to learn that using a three-word phrase will get you connected approximately 20% of the time. I learned this powerful question from listening to executive secretaries calling company executives to relay important information.

I suggest that you do take a moment to think about what the three words might be before you continue reading. Okay? Please, pause for a moment. Please think about what this phrase might be before you continue reading. You are more likely to appreciate and use this deceptively simple, powerful phrase. (It is bolded in the following dialogue.)

Scenario 1

Executive Secretary

Mr. Marshall's office.

You

Is he in?

Executive Secretary

(Transferring the call.) Yes, he is.

What do you do when you are not connected immediately? Here is one way to maximize your chances of scheduling an appointment:

Scenario 2

Executive Secretary

Mr. Marshall's office.

You

Is he in?

Executive Secretary

He's in a meeting, I expect him to be free around 3:30.

You

I'll call back, thank you.

Executive Secretary

May I tell him you called?

You

(Agreeably) Sure. (Reflective)
Maybe you can help me out-I'm
not sure I should be speaking with
Mr. Marshall. *(Faster, and with
enthusiasm)* The company I'm
with sells postage meters and
parcel shipping systems. Would
that sort of thing fall into Mr.
Marshall's area?[8]

Please examine what transpired in the
two scenarios. In Scenario One, you were
connected, almost effortlessly. Perhaps
the Executive Secretary thought you were
someone else. Perhaps she just reacted to
the brevity of your request. Possibly, the
tone of your voice was authoritative.
Perhaps all three factors were working in
your favor.

Scenario Two is more typical. The
Executive Secretary immediately
responds by providing information.

---

[8]Notice how similar this is to, "Would that fall into
your area of responsibility?"

Instead of asking him to return your call, say that you'll call back. Doing his job, the secretary asks who is calling. You amiably reply, "Sure," but you insure interest on the secretary's part by asking if he can help you. You then succinctly and truthfully explain the reason for your call and ask, "Would that sort of thing fall into Mr. Marshall's area?"

It is just possible that Mr. Marshall does not, handle this area. This is a more typical scenario:

Executive Secretary

Not really. Mary Lantz, our Director of Facilities Management is in charge of that, or you might want to talk to Bob Ellis, he runs the Mailroom and reports to Mary.

Look at what happened. Instead of calling back someone who is difficult to reach because he is constantly in meetings, you uncovered the correct contact names.

Consider finding out the Executive Secretary's name and then asking to be transferred to him or her. Once transferred, you might introduce yourself as follows:

You

Mr. Lantz, my name is Bruce Silver.
We've never spoken if you're trying to
place me, but Mr. Marshall's office
suggested that I touch base with you.
(Brief pause) The company I'm with sells
postage meters and mailing machines.
Would that sort of thing fall into your
area of responsibility?

Please take a moment to examine the
results of the last dialogue. In Scenario
One, you gain immediate access. In
Scenario Two, you gain leveraged entree
to Mr. Lantz. Both are good results,
particularly for such a short, easy-to-use
technique.

Following are phrases that may find
helpful when speaking with
administrative assistants, and other
support personnel:

- Would you know? Is
  _____ _____ in
  today?

- Maybe you could help me.

- Sometime over the next six months or so, I'd like to earn _____'s business.

- I'll touch base with _____ later, thanks.

- Who would handle that sort of thing?

- I could send _____ a one-page fax, so he'd have it in front of him when he calls me back. *(Brief pause)* How do you feel about that?

- What's the best fax number to use?

- I was speaking with
  _____
  about _____
  ago. We were talking about
  _____.

- Would you know, what's happening concerning _____?

- When would be the best time to touch base?

- You may remember,
  _____
  were talking about
  _____.
  I haven't been able to get a hold of her lately. Would you know her

feelings about that, *or would she be available?*

- Could you ask

  _____ _____

to give me a call, please?

APPENDIX 3 - USING VOICEMAIL AND AUTOMATED ATTENDANTS TO YOUR ADVANTAGE

A number of cost-cutting drives over the last twenty-five years have ushered in many changes in technology and staffing levels.

Once, when you called a company an Operator / Attendant always answered the phone. Today, that is a rarity. In an effort to boost profits, tens of thousands of employees were laid off or encouraged to retire early as a result of corporate re-engineering and restructuring. The trend started some time ago. Evidence this quote from the September 14, 1992 edition of *Forbes Magazine:*

This year's economy has disappointed workers, central bankers and sales executives. . . . Corporations have done so much trimming of staffs and costs that they could see very good earnings gains even with a small rebound in sales.[9]

One of the ramifications of this deep cost cutting is the reduction of secretarial staff by automation. Computerized systems frequently answer the phones. These are called automated attendants. Computerized systems also take messages. These are called voicemail. A prospect's voicemail system can be a major obstacle, or if you take advantage of it, a useful too. Here are a few insights and suggestions for taking advantage of voicemail systems:

- If you are transferred to the voice mail system on the first phone ring, the person you are calling is

---

[9]Steedley, Gilbert, "Room for Optimism," *Forbes*, September 14, 1992, Volume 150, Number 6, p. 540.

likely to be on their phone. You can always hang up and call back later.

- In many systems, you can get out of the voicemail by hitting "O" for Operator.

- You usually can drop out of the system. Then, you may speak with an operator or coworker. Usually, this is done by dialing "O," or a four-digit extension, sometimes followed by a # sign.

- When you get stuck in voicemail, dial "O" for Operator, explain that you've been getting your prospect's voicemail and then ask

- If your contact is free

- For your contact's administrative assistant's extension

- For the name and extension of another contact.

- Leave a message, transfer out of the system by pushing someone's extension number, explain that you have already left a message on your prospect's voicemail. Find out whether your prospect is in today. If he or she is in, ask a question like, "What's the best way to touch base with her today?"

- When frustrated by a machine that answers the telephone and requires that you enter an extension number, do what it wants. It is only a machine.

Most companies with automated attendants have four-digit telephone extension. Punch in a four digit number. (Some systems require that you hit a pound sign afterwards. If nothing happens, pause a moment and hit the "#" button.) When the automated attendant connects to you someone, ask them for the extension of the person with whom you want to speak.

Hint: If the person that you've been transferred to by an automated attendant answers their extension with their name, simply repeat their name with a question, "Mary Johnson?" When they reply, "yes," continue with something like, "Oh, I was trying to reach Martha Green." The chances are they will look up the extension number and transfer the call.

APPENDIX 4 - CONVERTING "NO'S" INTO OPPORTUNITIES

Wouldn't it be wonderful if every time you picked up the phone and called someone, you got through and they bought? Maybe, but if so, there is a good chance that your job would pay a lot less money. (After all, it would be a low-skill job.)

You are not going to schedule an appointment every time you speak with someone. You may have better results contacting some prospects two or three times before asking for an appointment. (People are usually more willing to buy from someone with whom they are comfortable. Two ways to make someone feel comfortable are to show that you have staying power and that you are interested in their business.)

Realizing and planning for a multiple-call sales cycle prevents disappointment and frustration. If you realize that you may alienate your prospect by continuing to ask for an appointment, change your tact. Rephrase your prospect's reasons for saying, "no." Make sure you understand his or her rationale, then jot yourself a note explaining exactly why your contact is not currently interested in getting together.

Armed with this information, when you do call back, remind your prospect of your last conversation, and follow up with one of these phrases:

- I thought I'd get you some information that we didn't have a chance to discuss last time we spoke.

- I just wanted to bring you up to speed on what I've been doing on my end. *(Describe any actions you are taking. Be positive.)*

- I sent you information a while back. If you forget it perhaps we need to get together so I can get you something that's really relevant.

- Hi, Who would I speak with about ___ <brief product description>___, things like that.

- The company I'm with competes with _<major competitor>__ for __<brief product description>___. Would that sort of thing, be your area of responsibility?[10]

- Who do you feel I should speak with about that?

- I'm with

_____,

---

[10]Use this when you need to establish credibility, and the competition has it.

the company that handles your

_____.

Who would I speak with? *(Rapidly followed by)* Who works with it most often?[11]

- (To eliminate annoyance when you did not get the correct spelling of someone's name) Oh, that's such a simple name, and I didn't hear it.

- *(As an alternate for "Is he in?")* I'm looking for _____, please.

---

[11]This phrase assumes that you have the company as a client, and that your company has more than more product or service to sell.

- Maybe you can help me out, just on a general question.

- Is it possible? Would you be able to give me some insight into whether anyone there can use my ____products or services_____?

- Have you heard about anyone or anything that might show a future need?

The information that you glean when you make inquiries often pays off handsomely.

This page is for your thoughts, drawings, poems, *etc.*

This page is for your thoughts, drawings, poems, etc.

A SPECIAL FEATURE FOR THE KINDLE EDITION.

Amazon allows authors to update Kindle books. I plan to update the Kindle version of this book based upon feedback from readers and to provide free updates. Sign up here to be advised when I update the book. I am using Mail Chimp to send the updates. You may unsubscribe at any time.

http://eepurl.com/ZKT15

Or, send an email to aherbertjordan@bigbusinessbenefits.com

You can manually download the updated versions, or tell Amazon to automatically update when I issue an updated version. (See

http://www.amazon.com/gp/help/customer /display.html?nodeId=201252670)

(The Kindle edition, is available at a nominal cost through Amazon's MatchBook program.)

HOW DID I DO?

The most important thing that I can do as an author is to stay in touch with my reader's needs and desires.

Please let me know your thoughts by sending an email to aherbertjordan@bigbusinessbenefits.com.

Persuasion Magic is also available in a print version. It is available on Amazon.com and in most bookstores.

Please visit http://bbb.max-opp.com/SignUp to register for free updates to this book and receive occasional special offers and information about my latest books.

ABOUT THE AUTHOR

Visit http://www.AHerbertJordan.com to learn more about my sales-oriented books and modules.

I also write non-business books under the name of Alan H. Jordan. Please see http://www.AlanHJordan.com.

My picture book, *The Monster on Top of the Bed,* comes in print, Kindle, iPad, Kobo and Nook editions.

Giving it as a gift to a prospect or client who has children or grandchildren is an inexpensive way to build rapport.

If your company wants to use it as a giveaway, a special sponsored edition can be prepared that features your company name, company logo and contact information. Visit http://www.Monbed.com to learn more, buy a copy, or request information about sponsoring an edition.

THANK YOU

I know you could have picked from dozens of books about sales and motivation, but you selected this one. So, a big thanks for buying *Persuasion Magic* If you liked what you've read, and you'd love others to benefit by tapping into their potential, I need your help.

Please take a moment to leave a review for this book on Amazon. This feedback will help me continue to write the kind of books that help you get the results you want. If you love *Persuasion Magic*, then please let me know.

If you happen to be active on any other websites or platforms, such as Goodreads, Shelfari, Facebook or Twitter I hope you'll be extra generous with your time and give this book a mention there too.

(Sign up here to be advised when I provide free updates. I am using Mail Chimp to send the updates. You may unsubscribe at any time. http://eepurl.com/ZKT15)

www.ingramcontent.com/pod-product-compliance
Lightning Source LLC
Chambersburg PA
CBHW021422170526
45164CB00001B/63